I0494890

Life Insurance And You!

Life Insurance and You

Demystifying the Issues

R. Nelson Letshwene

Copyright© R. Nelson Letshwene, 2015, 2017, 2018

All rights reserved. This book is intellectual property protected by international copyright law. No part of this publication may be reproduced in any form without the prior written permission of the author and publisher, except in brief quotations embodied in critical articles and reviews.

Published by Moedi Publishing, a division of Moedi Learning Technologies.
Gaborone, Botswana.
Pretoria, South Africa
©R. Nelson Letshwene
PO BOX 80927, Gaborone, Botswana
PO BOX 1766, Rustenburg, 0323, South Africa
nelslets@gmail.com / nelson@moedi.net
www.nelsonletshwene.com

Moedi Publishing

ISBN-13: 978-1985218123
ISBN-10: 1985218127 (CreateSpace-Assigned)
BISAC: Business & Economics / Insurance / Life

> "Better a little caution than a great regret"
>
> George S Clason
> *The Richest Man in Babylon*

DISCLAIMER:

This publication is designed to provide competent and reliable general information regarding the subject matter covered. However, it is published with the understanding that the author and publisher are not engaged in rendering legal, financial, or other professional advice through this medium. If legal, financial, or other expert assistance is required, the services of a professional should be sought. The author and publisher specifically disclaim any liability that is incurred from the use or application of the contents of this book.

Also, by R Nelson Letshwene

1. *The Money Field* – In the game of money, all are players, but some are more skilled than others.
2. *Seven Essential Money Skills* – Building a healthy relationship with your money
3. *My Money My Power* – How to lead your money through purposeful and decisive actions
4. *If We Were All #Financially Literate* – 49 virtues of financial knowledge
5. *Functional Mastery Over My Finances*
6. *Your Longing Is Your Calling* – How to find your purpose through the seven desires of life
7. *Faith and Purpose* – Living life to the full without fear, guilt, and regrets

Table of Contents

DISCLAIMER: vi

Preface 1

The Case for Life Insurance 5

What Is Life Insurance? 15

Why would you need life insurance? 21

What Determines Your Life Insurance Needs? 29
The Life Cycle 31

How Much Cover Should I Take? 35
What Am I Buying, At What Price? 40
How much will I claim? 42

Life Insurance for Your Partner 45
Family Matters 46
To Tell or Not to Tell? 47
The Secondary Breadwinner 49
How Can Businesses Retain Key Employees? 53

Designating a Beneficiary 55
Revocable and Irrevocable Beneficiaries 56
Primary and Contingent Beneficiaries 57
Multiple Beneficiaries 57
How Do You Name or Change A Beneficiary? 58
Why Designating the Proper Beneficiary Is
Important? 60

Life Insurance and Terminal Illness 63

Can You Purchase Additional Life Insurance?........ 64
Loan Against A Policy? 67

Disclose Medical History 71
Are Life Insurance Medical Exams Going Away?... 75

The Underwriting Process 77
How do insurance companies classify term insurance applicants?.. 78
What Factors Go into The Underwriting Process? 83
Where Does the Insurance Company Get Its Information?... 85
What is the purpose of the underwriting process? 87
Once my policy is approved, will I have to go through the underwriting process again?................ 89

Life Insurance Benefits 91
Where to Look? 94
Individually Owned Life Insurance Policies............. 95
Group life insurance policies 96
Employer-Based Group Life Insurance 97
Accidental Death Policy 98
Travel Accident Insurance... 99
Mortgage Life Insurance...100
Credit life insurance 101
Waiver of Premiums on Death.....................................103

The Claiming Process...................................... 105
How Should You Receive the Life Insurance Proceeds?..108

The Life Insurance Professional 111

Credit Life Insurance: Good Deal or Rip Off? . 121

What is Credit Life insurance? 121
Who Is Protected? 123
Can I Cede My Term Insurance Policy Instead?.. 125
What If You Repay Your Loan Before Its Term?. 131

Examples of Ancillary Benefits...................... 133
ACCIDENTAL DEATH BENEFITS.............................. 134
Accidental Death Cover... 135
Commuter Cover.. 136
Capital Disability Benefit... 137
Dread Disease Cover 138

Bibliography 140

Other Books by Nelson Letshwene 141

ABOUT THE AUTHOR..................................... 145

Preface

Life Insurance is not a product you can pick off the shelf when you need it, and pay at the till. You can't order it at point of need and have it delivered overnight.

But it is a tool you need to have before you need it. And it must be adequate. It is a protection tool. It can be used to protect your assets and your business. It can be used to protect your family and loved ones. It can be used to shield you against unintended consequences.

The trick is that you'll never know when you will need it. You can't time the need and buy it just in time.

Why do people who need insurance go uninsured? Who can afford to go without life insurance? Is it a product for everyone? Is it about affordability? Is there missing knowledge and understanding? Is there lack of ability to assess the personal risks that can be covered through insurance? Is there an attitude problem? Is it the case of 'bad things won't happen to me' syndrome?

Whatever the case may be, it is important to answer all of these questions and to demystify all issues around life insurance.

This book is for both the insurance buyer and the seller. It will help the buyer know what they are buying, and it will help the seller explain better some things that go unexplained in the sales experience.

Acknowledgement:

The last chapter of my first book, *Functional Mastery Over My Finances*[1], was entitled, Life Insurance and You!

That chapter has grown into this complete book that you have in your hands today.

---

[1] R. Nelson Letshwene, Functional Mastery Over My Finances, Reach Publishers, 2008

I got involved in the insurance industry in 2000, and since life insurance is a major part of personal finance, even after 'leaving' the industry by closing my agency, I have never really left the sector. Having written many articles, and having facilitated many workshops on the subject, I'm back with this book, for both the client and the broker.

Thank you for taking your time to go through this book. You will be glad you did.

Thank you

Nelson Letshwene

February, 2018

The Case for Life Insurance

This is an ordinary pair of shoes...

They could belong to anyone – BUT ...

... <u>Suppose They were yours</u>?

... Empty shoes – You, no longer here, having passed on to the world that needs no shoes ...

Who would fill in these shoes? They may not seem like big shoes, but what responsibilities did they carry?

At any point in our lives, we have to stop and answer the "should you die?" question.

Life does not end when yours ends. Who would pay the bills that always arise when someone passes on? Would those you leave behind have the money to do it? Or would they have to scrimp and save – and go without things they need – for months, perhaps even years, after your departure, just to get these bills paid off?

Dear friend,

I know that you are interested in life insurance. I know that you know how important it is. I know this because I know that no one in their right mind would want their loved ones to have economic struggles if they could do something about it.

But I want to ask you a pointed (and perhaps indiscreet) question:

Are you satisfied with what you have done about it?

Note that I am not asking if you have done anything about it. I am asking if you are *satisfied* with what you have done?

I'm sorry if that question seems blunt. (Or Am I?)

Now, here is a question that you might not frown at: do you know enough about life insurance to be able answer the above questions?

Most people would say, but how

can I know if what I have done is enough? And I would say, that is a very good question.

This book will hopefully bring you to the point where you will be able to answer that question to your satisfaction.

If you are satisfied with what you have done, good. Your question would most probably then be: how would I go about claiming, or informing my loved ones on what they need to do to claim my insurance benefits at the right time?

You see, every year millions of dollars are left unclaimed in insurance companies the world over because clients don't know where to look, or what processes to follow.

So, the claiming process, which we will also cover in this book, is vitally important to the whole insurance business.

Otherwise, what would be the point of going through all the trouble of getting insured, and then no one that you had intended to benefit, claiming the benefits?

Consider that it can be difficult for your family when you are gone. No one can replace you. And yet, something can carry on where you left off. They have certainly appreciated how you have provided for them all along the way all the years of your life. Why should they not keep right on appreciating you when you are gone – remembering that you, at least, shall have given them a chance to start out even in life?

If you died tomorrow, (here I should say, 'God forbid', right?), there could be all kinds of issues, among which are bills:

- Doctor bills for final sickness
- Hospital bills for related expenses
- Funeral service expenses
- Burial plot and tomb stone
- Unpaid taxes

And these are payable immediately upon your death. The lingering expenses include:

- School fees for your children
- Regular unpaid monthly accounts such as
    - utilities,
    - monthly groceries,
    - clothing for your growing children,
    - housing expenses,
    - unsecured loans
    - Credit cards
    - Etc.

And the list doesn't stop here!

You may be taking it for granted that you have an income and you are able to pay for these expenses now. But think about it – who would pay, should you die?
Wouldn't it be comforting to your family if you had made arrangements in advance to help take care of these expenses?

To help you do this, I want to arm you with knowledge. No, don't get me wrong, I am not about to sell you an insurance policy now, after all, you may have all the policies you need right now. I would just like to give you conviction. I would like to empower you by giving you the knowledge you need and hopefully you will go out and get a policy to meet your particular needs, if that need becomes apparent.

Maybe you did buy a policy but you are not convinced to keep it. You see, another thing that often happens is that a person may have a policy for years without anything happening. And then they decide to cancel it, and then something happens that requires a policy.

Yes, we should also talk about your concerns about insurance companies and insurance people. What is your perception of the insurance industry and its people?

Allow me to demystify life insurance. In this book, we give you the chance to understand this concept that could save you and your family heartaches and sorrows.

We go from understanding the agent that sells the policy to you

... to filling in the proposal form - and knowing that it is only that – a proposal.

... to the suitable policy for your needs.

... we talk about nominating a beneficiary or beneficiaries.

... we talk about the importance of disclosing medical history

... to the cover and peace that follows

... we talk about claiming life insurance benefits – what processes to follow; where to look for other policies that you might not know about that have nominated you as a beneficiary.

... and much more ...

These are the features you will find in this book. If this chapter has already seemed like a lot to read, it's because there is a lot to say ...

But with it, is a way for you to spare your family some of the tears and heartaches and sorrow that your death would cause.
You do know the value of life insurance. You are interested in your family's welfare.
So – let me ask you once again – are you satisfied that you have done enough?
Remember – there is no such thing as a second chance after you are gone. What you do for your family, you must do now – not tomorrow, not next week, not next year – but today.

Don't let ignorance be the stumbling block ... because at the end, dear friend, ignorance is not bliss ...

That is why I hope you will keep on reading – to arm yourself with knowledge of this all-important subject.

You will always be glad you did.

What Is Life Insurance?

No matter how diligently you build your financial empire, failure to purchase sufficient insurance can leave you in a desperate position in a heartbeat!

You hope you never need it, but should the need arise, you'd be glad if it's there.

When you buy a car, you make sure it is insured before you even drive it out of the shop floor, in fact, the bank won't let you drive off unless your ...err I mean, ... *their* asset is insured.

Why? Because common sense tells you that failure to insure it may put you in an anxious position within a blink of an eye! Some reckless driver may change your plans in a flash!

We protect what we value the most: the car, the house and house contents.

The idea of insuring what we value, including our own lives, is not a new concept. In fact, you could go on the internet on Wikipedia[2] and study the history of modern insurance from its official inception in the 18th century. You will find that the desire to protect ourselves, our properties, and loved ones against loss from risks in life is as old as humanity itself.

While there is a lot of information on this subject that you could find, in this book I would only like to make a case

---

[2] www.wikipedia.org

for personal insurance.

Isn't it funny how we may insure all the material things in our lives, but forget the most important element: The owner!? All your possessions are insured, but are you insured?

If your car gets involved in an accident, you can replace it if it is insured. If a thief breaks into your house and steals your possessions, you can replace them, if they're insured.

Well, what about you? If you are involved in some accident, can you afford to get yourself repaired? (Hospital costs). What if you are a "write-off"? – Well, people are never written offs, but I mean you can't continue to do the things you used to do before. You are a "write-off" at your work. Redundant. No longer needed! Will you have enough money to continue on living?

This is where personal insurance comes in! Now let's be frank. Many people never bother about making provision for their future, and end up regretting it. You think, when I get a better salary, I will start a savings account. You know what? Better salaries never come!

Back to the issue at hand: what must I protect myself against? What are the risks?

The collective name for life insurance, disability cover and trauma cover is "risk cover". Risk cover means protecting yourself against the risks in life. You therefore insure yourself against anything that could happen to you, and work to your financial disadvantage. This includes disability, accidents, traumas such as illness, and even death.

With life insurance you protect yourself and your family against the risk of dying suddenly. Life insurance is an agreement between you (the insured) and an insurer. Under the terms of a life insurance contract, the insurer promises to pay a certain sum to someone (a beneficiary) when you die, in exchange for your premium payments.

Your job is to keep your end of the deal by paying your premiums. Upon your death, your beneficiaries need to know what to do to claim their benefits. The insurer should then keep their end of the deal and pay your beneficiaries accordingly.

3

Why would you need life insurance?[3]

The most common reason for buying life insurance is to replace the income lost when you die.

By buying life insurance, you are essentially providing your beneficiaries with a financial person who will be there to continue to do what you used to do, at least financially, when you

---

[3] This chapter was originally published in brief in the book, *Functional Mastery Over My Finances*, Reach publishers, 2008, and in *Seven Essential Money Skills*, Moedi Publishing, 2015.

are no longer there.

Let us look at six more reasons for life insurance to add to this one.

Secondly, another common use of life insurance proceeds is to pay off any debts you leave behind to avoid causing financial problems for your family. Many traditional loans do come with "automatic" credit life cover, so they should be covered if you died before you could pay them off. The concerning debts are unsecured debts or informal loans even if they are used for more regular assets such as building a house, buying a car, or some other assets. Credit card debts and medical bills that are not covered by medical aid are often left unpaid when someone dies. These obligations must be paid from the assets left behind. This can deplete the resources that your family needs.

Life insurance can be used to

pay off these debts, leaving your other assets intact for your family to use.

Thirdly, Life insurance provides liquidity to your estate. That is, it provides cash. If you were to die now, would it be possible for the estate duty to be paid in cases where it is due? You may leave some liquid assets such as cash, and savings, and some illiquid assets such as real estate, vehicles, and maybe shares. Your liquid assets may not be enough to pay all the debts that you leave behind, plus all the expenses that arise because of your death such as funeral expenses and estate taxes. Your illiquid assets may have to be sold in order to meet these obligations when they come due. This may cause a financial loss if the assets must be sold cheaply in order to get the money on time. Life insurance can avert this situation, because the proceeds are available almost immediately upon your death.

Fourthly, Life insurance creates an estate for your heirs. After your debts and expenses are paid, there may not be much left over for your family. Life insurance can automatically provide assets for them after your death. You may also deliberately use life insurance as an inheritable asset for your heirs by naming them as beneficiaries. Even if you don't need life insurance to cover any debts, if you think you don't have any assets that your heirs can inherit, you can set them up with life insurance that they will inherit.

Fifth, Life insurance can be a critical component for specialized business applications, such as funding a buy-sell agreement. Under a buy-sell agreement, life insurance can be used to provide cash for the purchase of a deceased owner's interest in the business. People in partnerships can take life insurance on each other's lives so that they can buy their partner out without having to dissolve the business.

Life insurance can also be used to insure "key persons" in your business. Upon the death of a key person, it may take a long time and resources to train other people to keep the business profitable. Key person insurance would provide the funds to train such new people.

Sixth, Life insurance may also be a great way to give to charity when you die. You may have always had a great philanthropic desire, but not the means to make it a reality. Life insurance can do that for you. By naming your favourite charity as a beneficiary on a policy, you are ensuring that you can contribute to courses that you care about.

You may even use it to start a foundation such as an education foundation for your children and relatives, or contribute to an existing foundation, university, or institution.

Finally, life insurance can be an investment vehicle. Although this may not be the primary use of insurance, many people feel that they are pouring money into a source from which they might not benefit personally. As a result, many insurance products, especially term life insurance products, have a maturity value where a person can benefit while they're still alive.

Some types of life insurance policies may actually make money for you, as well as provide the benefits described above. Most universal policies have an investment portion attached to them. This can help you with long-term financial goals.

Many companies now have a return of premiums after a certain period has elapsed without a claim. This way, people don't feel that they have lost their money by paying premiums for years without benefit.

What Determines Your Life Insurance Needs?

Your life insurance needs change as your life changes.

When you are young, you may not have a need for life insurance, especially if you have no dependents and responsibilities other than to yourself. However, as you take on more responsibility and your family grow, your life insurance needs increase. Your life insurance needs increase mostly in proportion to the dependents you get along the way of life. You should periodically review your needs in order to ensure that your life insurance coverage adequately reflects your life situation.

The basic issues that determine your life insurance needs are factors such as your age, your general state of health, and your life-style.

At a younger age, with the best general state of health, your premiums would be very low, and these would increase as you grow older, and your general state of health declines. A rigorous life-style may add risk to your life and thus may attract premium loading when you take life insurance.

The Life Cycle

As human beings we go through the cycles of life. At each point, our needs would change. Let us look at some of these stages in the life cycle.

No-Attachment Youth

As long as you are still dependent on someone else, chances are, no one else is dependent on you. At this point in your life you really may have no need for life insurance. No attachment means that you have no dependents and therefore have no *insurable interest*. Insurable interest should however not only be looked at in terms of your dependents, but insurable interest exists when you derive a financial or other benefit from the existence or continuation of a thing or an event. For example, regardless of your age, you may start a career such as being a musician or artist early, and may wish to insure your voice from which you derive a benefit.

So, regardless of your age, you may still take life insurance and you could name a beneficiary of your choice like a charity.

Family and Career

When you raise a family and are focussed on your career, it may be the time you need the most insurance. You need to carefully consider all types of cover and carry the most optimum.

At this stage, education policies for children should be put into effect. You get protected against all types of risks as may be applicable to you such as accidental death, dread disease cover, etc. – some of which are discussed in this book.

Pre-retirement

At pre-retirement, your insurance needs may have

diminished somewhat, with a great focus on your medical insurance and less on covering for dependents. Another evaluation with a financial planner may be necessary to make sure that you stay protected. Throughout your life, the thing being tracked for insurance purposes is insurable interest. As long as that exists, you may need life insurance.

Your goal may be to settle your mortgage so that at retirement you have a place you can call your own. Depending on the size of your estate, you may need to think about insurance to cover estate duty when you die.

Retirement

At retirement, your biggest needs are mostly medical and not so much on dependents. The term policies you had taken when you were much younger will be maturing and you can use the funds to take medical cover or to settle all your debts, or do the things you had put off until retirement.

Life insurance needs don't cease to exist just because you are in retirement. Remember, as long as you have insurable interest, you should stay insured. Your financial planner is your partner in planning for your financial future and all the cycles of your life.

How Much Cover Should I Take?

There are several methods that you can use to estimate your life insurance need.

The determination of the amount of cover you take is very important since that informs your premiums. Just about every insurance company would have calculators on their websites and their applications, which makes it easier for you to arrive at a figure, and therefore the amount of premiums you need to contribute.

There are also traditional methods that are used to determine the amount of cover you should have.

These calculations are sometimes referred to as "rules of thumb" and can be used as a basis for your discussions with your insurance professional.

First, is The Income rule, which is the most basic rule of thumb. This states that your insurance need would be equal to 6 or 8 times your gross annual income. Knowing the amount of cover you should have, your insurance professional will work with you to compute the amount of premiums you should contribute for that level of cover over the term of the cover. For example, a person earning a gross annual income of 100 000 bucks should have between 600 000 and 800,000 in life insurance coverage.

While that may seem like a lot of money to some people, when you compute a mortgage and car payments alone, you know it may not even be enough, not to say anything about living expenses for your beneficiaries.

Your home loan or mortgage and your car loan may already be covered by a separate credit life insurance and you may not need to provide for them under your general life insurance cover.

Second, is The Premiums as percentage of income.

Under this rule of thumb, also commonly used, a minimum of six to ten percent of your gross income (as the primary income earner) should be spent on life insurance premiums. Add an additional one percent for each dependent. Once you determine the percentage of your income which should be spent on life insurance premiums, you should purchase as much life insurance as you can get for that premium amount.

Using a similar example to the above, a person with an annual gross income of 600'000 bucks has to set aside between 36'000 and up to 60'000 per year for insurance, or a monthly premium of between 3'000 and 5'000. What can you get for this amount?

Don't assume that all insurance companies sell the same cover for the same amount of premiums. It is important to get quotations from different companies to see how much cover you can get for the amount of premiums you are prepared to pay.

You can divide your premium to make sure that all areas such as disability cover, dread disease cover, accidental death, funeral cover, and even waiver of premiums on disability, etc. are covered. With good advice from your insurance professional, you can get a lot of mileage out of this premium.

Third, Income plus expenses.

This rule considers your insurance need to be equal to 5 times your gross annual income plus the total of any mortgage, personal debt, final expenses, and special funding needs (i.e., child's education). For example, assume that you earn a gross annual income of 600'000 and have expenses that total 200 000. Your insurance need would be equal to 3'200'000 (i.e. 600'000 x 5 + 200,000).

Finally, there are several more comprehensive methods used to calculate life insurance need. Overall, these methods are more detailed than the rules of thumb and provide a more complete view of your insurance needs. This is where your insurance professional comes in. Just remember that almost all life insurance coverage requires medical examinations. We will discuss this in subsequent pages.

What Am I Buying, At What Price?

The above methods help you to arrive at the price you would pay for your insurance.

It is important to consider not just the premium (price) you are paying, but the cover that you are buying at that price.

The insurance business is largely a numbers' game. It is in the interest of the insurance company to get large pools of people in the preferable risk group because these would likely not claim as much as substandard groups. The larger the groups, the more affordable, or lower the premiums are likely to be for everyone in the group, depending on claim statistics and profitability.

It is also important for you as a client to be part of a large group, which will help you to lower your premiums for a much larger cover amount.

If insurance companies are competing on price (i.e. low premiums), it is important for you as a client to not just look at the price for the cover you are getting.

You must look at their claim procedures and their claim success versus their repudiation rates.

Smaller companies still building their pools may charge less in premiums in order to attract more people, but have much longer waiting periods, and have a much more rigorous claims procedure, which may lead to your claim being repudiated.

How much will I claim?

The amount of cover you carry is the amount you will get paid by the insurance company when the *insured event* occurs. Life cover pays out in the event of the death of the insured.

If the insured does not die, and the policy reaches its maturity date, then only the investment value gets paid out, not the sum assured. So, for a term insurance policy of say 20 years, it will pay the insured amount if the insured dies at any time within the 20 years. If it reaches maturity without the death of the insured, then the insured will get the invested portion of the policy, not the sum assured. This will most likely be less than the sum assured.

Sometimes people would complain that the insurance companies are cheating them because they were "promised" millions of bucks as the sum assured, but upon the maturity of the policy they only got an amount less than that. That is because they confuse the *sum assured* and the *investment portion*. The sum assured is only payable upon the occurring of the *insured event*, which is death.

Remember that if you died in the seventh month immediately after the waiting period where applicable, of say six months, the whole sum assured would be paid out regardless of the fact that you shall have paid only seven months' worth of premiums.

6

Life Insurance for Your Partner

What remedy is there for the loss of a very valuable partner in life or in business?

Life throws many curve balls at us which demand that we should always be prepared. Your partner in family or business is that one who keeps the other part of you balanced. Without them, life can seem to come to a standstill.

There are solutions that

businesses can use to protect themselves against the loss of valuable partners. Families can apply the same solutions to family issues, when a valuable partner dies or is disabled.

Family Matters

The whole idea behind having a partner is for support, both emotionally and of course materially. Interestingly, material support may not even be in the form of money, but in the form of material help in your life.

We live in an age of insecurity where divorce and separations come easier than they did in the past. Partners may marry out of community of property and live together peacefully until the point of divorce, where one partner may realise that they have nothing to their name.

Life insurance is a material solution to dealing with the risk of losing a valuable partner in life. Money from life insurance can go a long way in helping to close the material gaps left by a partner. Of course, you can't take a policy to insure against divorce, but when you have a policy with surrender value, it might come handy when you need it most.

The key is always to remember not to steal from your future self. That means you should not cash or surrender a policy where the risk for which it was taken still exists.

To Tell or Not to Tell?

In relationships without trust however, it is almost a taboo to inform your spouse that you have insurance on their life, lest you die mysteriously for the sake of the insurance money.

There was a well-publicised case in which a psychiatrist[4] poisoned his wife for a slow death in order to claim the life insurance money. He is currently serving life sentence.

In another case, Dr Omar Sabadia[5] took a R2.9 million life insurance on his wife, and then "staged" a hi-jack where his wife died so that he could claim the insurance money. Fortunately, the police and the insurance company did thorough investigations and the man was caught and convicted of murder.

That has led to many people not wanting to talk about insurance to their partners.

In a relationship of trust however, this should not be a problem, weather this be at

---

[4] https://en.wikipedia.org/wiki/Colin_Bouwer .

[5] https://mg.co.za/article/1996-03-08-sabadia-murder-reveals-more-than-just-a-body

home or in business. Insurance should never be seen as a get rich quick scheme. If a person does not want to tell others about it, they could put it in their last will and keep it with their attorney. It is better to have it than not to have it.

The Secondary Breadwinner

Insuring the life of the main breadwinner in a family against death, disability, or any other interruption to the income stream, seems obvious. But often the financial problems caused by losing a secondary breadwinner are overlooked - and more often than not, the case of the stay-at-home parent bringing up children is ignored altogether. There are compelling reasons why the lives of *both* "senior partners" in a family unit should be insured.

To make it equitable, both partners can take equal insurance on each other's lives in the case where both partners are earning an income, and make each other beneficiaries.

Sometimes parents make minor children beneficiaries, forgetting that the money may not be available until the children have reached the age of maturity. There might therefore be a financial struggle in the presence of money.

While it is obvious to insure the main breadwinner in the family, consider the value of the unsung heroines who are today's domestic executives, running the home ever so effectively, without a steady income.

What problems could the death or disability of the stay-at-home partner bring to the family? Losing a home-maker or care-giver will involve a financial burden: apart from the cost of replacing these unsung "domestic services", the surviving partner may well have to reduce working hours or down-shift jobs in any event.

Would that be desirable? Would the remaining partner be able to afford quality education for the children and maintain the same quality of lifestyle?

A secondary income *can* make a serious difference to disposable income: losing it may well involve adverse lifestyle changes for the surviving spouse and children.

The costs of death (including not just the funeral, but winding up the deceased's estate) may well surprise you - especially if for any of many personal or business reasons, the deceased spouse was the legal owner of any property, which would need to be transferred to the surviving spouse.

A lump sum from an insurance policy, which pays out on death, can take care of this remarkably cost-effectively, without straining the remaining family finances.

Previously widowed partners who take children (or indeed aged parents or other relatives) into a second or subsequent marriage, should want to provide for their existing dependents' financial future, without having to rely on the goodwill or moral responsibility of the new spouse to look after those step-children and in-laws they may be inheriting! Besides, the new partner may have their own issues that they bring into the new relationship as well.

As you can see there are many ways to use insurance proceeds in life, as long as they are available when needed.

How Can Businesses Retain Key Employees?

In the same vein, businesses can use deferred compensation plans.

The employer and the employee may enter into a contract where the employer undertakes to provide an award to the employee on retirement by affecting an assurance contract.

This may be in addition to retirement benefits and serves as an added incentive for the employee to stay. The employer owns the contract, is the beneficiary and pays the contributions. Upon retirement or the agreed time period, the employer can cede this policy to the employee or surrender the policy and give the amount to the employee. Thus, the employee gets inflated benefits at retirement or death while in the service of the company.

Key-man insurance is an important part of business and there is more to say about it than in this short paragraph.

Business partners, in the same way, can take insurance contracts on each other's live to avoid their business being liquidated upon the death of the other.

If this all sounds a bit complicated, your financial adviser or broker will be glad to explain it to you in the context of your own circumstances. There is however no substitute for you taking the initiative to consider your own circumstances and plan for the future.

7

Designating a Beneficiary

A beneficiary is the person or entity you name (i.e., designate) to receive the death benefit of a life insurance policy.

Some companies may require that your beneficiary have an insurable interest in your life or be related to you (at least at the time the contract is initiated), while others have no such restriction.

If you do not want to name a person or entity as your beneficiary, you can name your own estate. The proceeds will then be distributed with your other assets according to your will. You should note, however, that naming your estate as beneficiary may have disadvantages. For example, in some instances, life insurance proceeds could be exempt from the claims of your creditors when there is a named beneficiary, but not when your estate is your named beneficiary.

Revocable and Irrevocable Beneficiaries

The beneficiary can be either revocable or irrevocable. A revocable beneficiary can be changed at any time. Once named, an irrevocable beneficiary cannot, by definition, be changed without his or her consent.

Primary and Contingent Beneficiaries

You can name as many beneficiaries as you want, subject to procedures set in the policy. The beneficiary to whom the proceeds go first is called the primary beneficiary. Secondary or contingent beneficiaries are entitled to the proceeds only if they survive both you and the primary beneficiary.

Multiple Beneficiaries

You may name multiple beneficiaries if you choose. There are no legal restrictions (and few company restrictions) on the number of beneficiaries you can designate.

If you name multiple beneficiaries, you must also specify how much each beneficiary will receive. You may not want to give each beneficiary an equal share, so you must state how the proceeds should be divided. Because of the numerous interest and dividend adjustments that the insurance company must make, the death benefit cheque often does not equal the policy's face value. So, it's wise to distribute percentage shares to your beneficiaries, or to designate one beneficiary to receive any residue or leftover balance.

How Do You Name or Change A Beneficiary?

When you buy life insurance, you will indicate your beneficiaries on the application. When changing a beneficiary, the insurer will provide you with a beneficiary designation form. Unless one or more of the beneficiaries is irrevocable, you only need to list the names of the beneficiaries, sign the form, and date it. Writing this on the change-of-beneficiary form will automatically revoke any previous designations. Be sure to check and update your beneficiary designations upon certain life events (e.g., divorce, remarriage, the birth of children, or death of beneficiaries).

Don't make the mistake of thinking that you can change your beneficiary in or through your will. Both the will and the insurance policy are only executed after your death. A change of beneficiary made in your will does not override the beneficiary designation of your life insurance policy. An insurance policy is a contract between the insurer and the insured, and the insurer is obligated to honour the contract by paying the proceeds to the named beneficiary. If you want to change the beneficiary of your life insurance, execute a change-of-beneficiary form. Do not rely on your will to do so.

Why Designating the Proper Beneficiary Is Important?

You should name both primary and contingent beneficiaries. If you have not named one or more beneficiaries, the proceeds pass to your estate at your death. Proceeds paid to your estate are subject to probate and will incur all of the expenses and delays associated with settling an estate. But named beneficiaries receive proceeds almost immediately after your death, and probate is bypassed. In addition, proceeds passing to your estate are subject to the claims of creditors and estate duty.

Other considerations when designating beneficiaries

If you become incompetent, you cannot name or change a beneficiary. You are considered incompetent only if you are legally declared to be so. The test is similar to the test regarding the making of wills or any other legal contract (i.e., do you have the capacity to understand your actions?).

It is not advisable to name a minor as a beneficiary unless you also appoint a guardian in your will or use a trust. If you do name a minor as a beneficiary, and you do not appoint a guardian or use a trust, the probate court will appoint a guardian for you.

Your right to change a beneficiary may be limited by a divorce decree or settlement agreement. In some cases, divorce allows a policy owner to change the beneficiary, even if the beneficiary is irrevocable. In other cases, the policy owner may be prohibited from changing the beneficiary or may be required to name a divorced spouse or children as irrevocable beneficiaries.

Life Insurance and Terminal Illness

If you are terminally ill, your life insurance policy is a valuable resource.

Not only can you use life insurance to provide adequate income to your survivors for their short- and long-term needs, but you also may be able to receive a portion of the death proceeds from your life insurance before you die in order to pay necessary expenses or to fulfil a dream.

Can You Purchase Additional Life Insurance?

When you are terminally ill, you pose an obvious risk to an insurance company, and you will probably be unable to buy additional life insurance coverage. However, some companies offer a guaranteed insurability rider when you purchase a life insurance and you may have to check if this option is available to you. Under a guaranteed insurability rider (additional purchase option), you may be able to buy additional life insurance without providing proof of medical insurability. If so, obtain the maximum coverage available.

Another way you can obtain additional cover is through your company's group life insurance program. If you are still employed, you may be able to purchase additional life insurance through your company's program with no evidence of medical insurability. Check with your company broker or agent.

If you are taking out a loan to buy a big-ticket item, and you are still employed, you may also be able to purchase credit life insurance that will pay off the balance of your loan when you die. For some reason most banks don't require a statement or declaration of good health when they issue out credit life insurance, just a statement of employment and that you have not been absent from work for a certain amount of time.

If you have just found out that you have a terminal illness, but you are relatively still in good health, you can approach some leading life insurance companies that have products that can give you life cover without excessive medical tests like HIV test. Such a product will depend on how long you live and thus how long you contribute. The amount of life cover increases with the years, to the effect that upon your death, you could have accumulated adequate cover for your dependents. Talk to your broker or agent about this.

If you have a life insurance policy or a pure endowment (savings) policy, you may add ancillary benefits like funeral cover to your already existing policy. Such additions don't always require medical tests. (Some, like dread disease cover may require medical tests).

As you already know, Life insurance can help provide adequate income to your survivors.

Life insurance can be used to help ensure estate liquidity. Buying as much life insurance as you can will help ensure that your estate has adequate cash available to pay for taxes and expenses that arise after you die, including the cost of a funeral, executor's fees, attorney's fees, debts, and the daily living expenses of your survivors.

Loan Against A Policy?

You may be able to take out a loan against the cash surrender value. If your life insurance policy has accumulated a cash value, you may be able to obtain a loan from the insurance company using your policy as collateral. The main disadvantage of taking a loan against your policy when you are terminally ill is that since it's unlikely you'll be able to repay it in full before your death, the loan balance will be subtracted from the proceeds that are payable to your beneficiaries. Also remember that a loan, by definition, charges interest. Your attitude should not be that you are using your own money, because the money that you are borrowing is not yours, but that of the insurance company. Yours will only be available upon your death, at which time the insurance company may lay a claim as your creditor.

You may be able to apply for benefits from a dread disease life insurance policy. This is usually a rider or an ancillary benefit attached to a life insurance policy that pays benefits to you when you are chronically or terminally ill. If you own dread disease life insurance, benefits will be paid to you while you are still living, and you can use the money you receive to pay your daily living expenses, increased medical costs, or in any other way you choose. However, the amount you receive (in the case of terminal illness, often 100% of the policy's face value) will reduce or eliminate benefits payable to your survivors.

You may want to sell your policy to a viatical settlement company or provider**. A viatical settlement is the sale of a life insurance policy to a third party, usually a viatical settlement funding company owned by a group of investors. When you sell your policy, you will generally receive between 40% and 85% of the face value of the policy, and you can use the cash payment any way you wish. Many individuals use the proceeds to pay medical costs or living expenses, while others use the proceeds to fulfil a final dream, or to experience the joy of giving money away to others. However, there are drawbacks. Your survivors will no longer be the beneficiaries of your life insurance policy, and they will

---

** This arrangement may not be currently available in all countries yet.

receive no money from the policy when you die.

One may envisage a sale of a policy only in a case where one no longer has any dependents. One should also ensure that the assets in your estate are more than the liabilities.

It is also important not to sell a policy where the risk for which it was taken still exists.

It is therefore important to seek counsel with a professional to make sure that you are not guided only by emotions or temporary situations that can be resolved in other ways other than sale of a policy.

9

Disclose Medical History

To ensure that claims on long-term insurance cover are assessed appropriately, it is necessary to disclose all information regarding medical background and conditions that are material to the risk in terms of an insurance policy.

The Long-term Insurance Act allows an insurance company to repudiate a claim if material information, that would have affected the risk assessment, is not disclosed at application stage.

The contract of long-term insurance is one of good faith and in this regard the disclosure of medical information must be honest, straightforward and complete in order to enable the insurer to appropriately assess the risk, says Joubert.

"Internationally all risk cover applications, whether life cover, disability cover, or dread disease cover are classified into either standard or substandard risk pools through a process of evidence based scientific underwriting," says Gerhard Joubert, executive director of the Life Offices' Association (LOA).

"The standard risk pool refers to people with no medical conditions, or other risk related factors, that adversely affect the risk of life, disability or dread disease cover on their lives. They will pay normal premium rates for the product involved.

All substandard risks, in other words, those with an expected increased mortality or morbidity, need to pay an actuarially calculated increased premium, referred to as a premium loading, in line with the added risk for the case in question."

Underwriters and medical doctors at insurance companies use sophisticated tables, based on sound medical evidence, to calculate the increased risk of each individual case.

It is therefore better for applicants to supply more, rather than less information. Disclosure of irrelevant information will have no impact on the underwriting process and it is better for the applicant to make all disclosures and not self-determine what is relevant. Full disclosures will prevent claims being turned down on the basis that material facts have not been disclosed.

For this reason, Joubert said it was advisable for all applicants to complete the medical questionnaires of the insurance company in their own handwriting. "This ensures that no questions are missed, misrepresented, or completed incorrectly. This can easily happen if somebody else completes these questions at a later stage for the applicant."

Even medical conditions that occurred in the past, for example lower back pain more than five years ago, should be mentioned. The onus is then on the life companies contracted to decide whether this information is relevant or not.

All information supplied to the insurer for underwriting purposes is totally confidential.

Are Life Insurance Medical Exams Going Away?

How is it that so many online insurance companies are able to sell insurance without requiring medical exams?

An article by Stamford Advocate[6], states: "Historically, the life insurance medical exam has been an important part of assessing risk – and it still is for people with various medical conditions and risk factors – but, in today's world, insurance companies have access to massive amounts of publicly available data that can help them calculate life expectancy with limited additional information. Examples of relevant data include your prescription drug history and

---

[6]http://www.stamfordadvocate.com/business/moneytips/article/Life-Insurance-Medical-Exams-Going-Away-12123720.php

motor vehicle records[7]. Predictive algorithms on life expectancy have advanced to the point that, for many applicants, insurance companies can correctly measure risk and underwrite policies without the need for a qualifying medical exam."

You must remember, however that being required to do a medical exam and disclosing medical information are two different things. The onus is still on you to disclose medical information, and the company, whether online or face to face, will decide whether to require a medical exam or not

---

[7] https://www.moneytips.com/bad-driving-can-affect-your-life-insurance-premiums

10

The Underwriting Process

When you submit an application for life insurance to an insurance company, the company goes through an underwriting process on your application.

This means that it will look at the information provided by you on the application form, (and obtain information from other sources such as your medical claim history, if necessary) in order to assess the risks associated with you as an individual. Your age, your occupation, your general state of health, your lifestyle and hobbies are some of the factors used to determine your risk factors. Based on the results of underwriting, the insurer will decide whether or not to sell you a term insurance policy.

It's not simply a matter of accepting or rejecting your application, though. Assuming the company deems you insurable, it will place you in a pool with other applicants who share similar characteristics and pose a similar degree of risk. This risk classification determines the premium you will pay for the term coverage you desire.

How do insurance companies classify

term insurance applicants?

According to Miller & Miller Insurance[8], upon the processing of your application form, you are likely to be classified into one of the following four risk groups: standard group, preferred group, substandard group, or uninsurable group.

Let us look into each of the groups and their implications on your application:

Standard risks: People in this group are individuals who, according to the insurance company's underwriting standards, can be covered without them having to pay a *rating surcharge* or being subjected to policy restrictions. A rating surcharge would be an additional rate on your premiums or conditions prior to your

---

[8] https://www.miller-miller.com/content/life/life-uw

application being accepted. Most people with a good general standard of health would fall in this group. The standard group with standard risks may be the largest group in the company.

Preferred risks: This group of applicants is made up of individuals whose life expectancy as a group is expected to be above average. This may be determined by medical exams and they may be found to be in greater state of health, without any such hazards as smoking and lack of exercise. For these, an insurance company would offer a lower than standard rate of premiums. One of the reasons for a lower rate is that since they tend to live longer, they would be paying their premiums for a longer time, and thus take care of the risk of dying too early under normal circumstances. They are preferred because the claims from this group would be lower or spread out over a much longer period, allowing the insurance company to remain profitable.

Substandard risks: This group is made up of individuals who, according to mortality tables, for health or other factors, cannot be expected (on average) to live as long as people who are not subject to the risk factors faced by the group. Risks may include less than optimal health with pre-existing conditions.

Some may be healthy but may be living risky lifestyles or engaged in dangerous or perceived dangerous occupations such as being in the army or with the police in volatile societies. Some may be involved in hazardous or dangerous sporting activities or pursuits such as high-speed sports, etc.

Substandard applicants are insurable, but only at higher than standard rates that reflect the added risk. Policies issued to substandard applicants are referred to as rated or extra risk policies.

***Uninsurable*:** These are applicants to whom an insurance company would refuse to sell term insurance because it would be unwilling to shoulder the added risks, which would fall outside their levels of insurable risks. From the underwriting process, an insurance company can decide that the risk factors associated with an applicant are too great or too numerous. It may be a combination of age, health, hazardous pursuits or location. Some locations may be prone to violence, which reduces life expectancy of residents of that location, or prone to certain health concerns or natural disasters.

In other cases, an applicant's circumstances may be so rare or unique, and register outside the company levels of preferred risk, that the company may have no basis to arrive at a suitable premium. They of course can't just charge any premium because they have to remain within affordable ranges. It would be cheaper for them and for an uninsurable client not to enter into the contract of insurance.

What Factors Go into The Underwriting Process?

The underwriting department of an insurance company would typically look at a number of factors during the underwriting process in order to evaluate an application in terms of risk. These factors enable the insurer to decide whether or not an applicant is insurable or not, and, if so, to place them into the appropriate risk group.

As has already been alluded to, some of the things considered are the potential insured's:

Age; Sex; Current health/physical condition; Personal health history; Family health history; Financial condition; Personal habits/character; Occupation; Hobbies, etc.

While these may be some of the primary factors, an insurance company can use more information about a client that may be accessible to it such as medical claim history, or other information accessible in general places like the internet. Online insurance companies use a lot of information accessible on the internet also, in addition to the information an applicant would supply on the online application process.

Where Does the Insurance Company Get Its Information?

An insurance company needs information in order to make an assessment about you, and it will gather information about you from several sources:

Your application or proposal form is the primary source: The basic source of underwriting information is your completed application form for term or any insurance product. This may be in written form on a paper form or online through an online application form. The questions on the application form are designed to give the insurer much of the information needed to make a decision. The company will then either reject your application, accept it and offer you insurance at a certain rate, or seek additional information. It is in the interest of both yourself and the insurance company that you give the most accurate and comprehensive information on your form.

Information from your agent/broker: In face to face applications, in many cases, the company would place great weight on the recommendations of your broker or insurance agent, particularly if your broker or agent has a good track record with the company. Because the broker or agent generally earn their living on commission, it is in their interest to make sure that they get insurable clients to avoid lapses in their policies. They might therefore be able to assess obviously severe economic or health conditions. An experienced insurance professional with good insights will know from initial interview whether a client is insurable or not.

Physical examinations: In life insurance, one of the primary factors in assessing risk is your health. So it's no surprise that one of the most important sources of underwriting information is a medical physical exam. After examining you, a physician selected by the insurance company supplies the company with a detailed medical report. This report generally tells the company all they need to know about your present health.

One of the reasons that online companies may be able to skip medical examinations is the availability of information online and, by your consent, may be able to get it directly from your physician or health practitioner.

What is the purpose of the

underwriting process?

Briefly, the purpose of term insurance underwriting is to spread risk among a pool of clients in a manner that is both fair to you and profitable for the insurer. Like other businesses, insurance companies need to make a profit. Therefore, it wouldn't make sense for them to sell term insurance to everyone who applies for it. Although they don't want to make you pay an excessively high rate, it would not be wise for them to charge all their policyholders the same premium. Underwriting enables the company to weed out certain applicants and to charge the remaining applicants premiums that are commensurate with their level of risk.

The underwriting process is therefore plays an important role in the insurance business.

Once my policy is approved, will I have to go through the underwriting process again?

It depends. Some policies will give you coverage without having to resubmit to the underwriting process, even if your risk factors have changed (e.g., your health has declined) since the company sold you the original policy.

If your policy doesn't contain this provision, you will have to virtually reapply for term insurance at certain intervals determined by your policy and undergo what is known as post-selection underwriting. At this time, the company has the right to deny you continued coverage. Even if they don't deny you insurance, it's likely they will at least put you in a higher risk group and raise your premium based on your increased age or changed circumstances.

Remember, though, if the company that wrote your original policy won't renew the policy or will do so only at a higher rate than you want to pay, shop around. Other companies may have less stringent underwriting standards, or perhaps larger pools of people in your category, which helps in spreading the risk. Smaller companies with smaller pools may be forced to be stringent in the beginning until their pools grow to an extend where the risk is carried by a lot more people.

11

Life Insurance Benefits

Life insurance benefits are not paid without human intervention.

If you are the beneficiary of a life insurance policy, obviously you must file a claim in order to receive any money. Often, this is as simple as contacting your insurance agent or company, and filling out some paperwork. However, if this is the only step you take, you may be missing out on other life insurance benefits to which you may be entitled. It is important to realise that there may be policies on which you are named as a beneficiary, which you may not be aware of.

Over the years and in many countries, lots of money go unclaimed from Insurance policies and pension funds because beneficiaries are not aware of them. Even you may have forgotten about a paid-up policy that may have matured.

In the case of pension funds, as soon as you reach retirement age, or you know of a loved one who has reached retirement age, you should go through every employer you have ever been engaged with to see if there wasn't any scheme that you were a part of, that the company may have contributed to in your name. You should also help those newly retired relatives who may not know how to ask the right questions in various places. We have mentioned earlier that sometimes relatives don't mention to their beneficiaries that they have been named as such on policies. So, when a loved one passes away, you may need to do some digging to find some policies.

Let us take some time to examine the types of policies from which you can claim, and subsequently, we will look at the claiming procedure.

Your spouse or family member may have owned one or more group policies that pay benefits depending on how the insured person died, or in restricted amounts. If you spend time uncovering these hidden policies, you may end up with a great deal more money from life insurance than you expected, or you may help minor children to uncover some hidden treasure from their parents. Beneficiaries may be minors and may not know to look, or where to look in the first place.

Where to Look?

Other than physical documents, you need to be aware that with an increase in telesales, many people have policies that they have agreed to via telephone calls from sales agents. In these cases, policies may be emailed to them and there might not be physical documents except the emailed copies. So, emails and electronic documents are important.

But one other evidence of contributions may be bank statements. By perusing through bank statements, you may find regular contributions as well as policy numbers where deductions were by debit order or stop orders. That may start a trace for you to find some unknown policies such as funeral policies and various other savings and investments.

Individually Owned Life Insurance Policies

Individually owned term or whole life policies are what most people think of as life insurance. These policies are purchased by one person, and pay benefits when the insured person dies. Your partner or family member may have owned one or more whole life or term life insurance policies. If your spouse or family member owned one of these policies, he or she probably kept it with his or her important papers, in a file, or in a safety deposit box. Lots of people keep these documents at their work place, so make sure that whoever cleans out the office gives you all the important personal belongings, which may include such policy documents. In this digital age, sometimes people don't keep physical copies but scanned copies. So, personal computers and cloud storage are also places to look. The challenge may be digital security like passwords, for which you may need a technology specialist to help you.

However, if you know that your spouse or family member owned an individual policy and you can't find it, call his or her insurance agent or company to check. Sometimes there is more than one agent or insurance company, or bank to call. An Identity Document and death certificate may be required.

Group life insurance policies

Group life insurance policies provide coverage to many people under one policy. Group insurance policies may be issued through an employer, bank, or other professional or social organizations, and they often pay benefits in specialised circumstances. Because the group holds the actual policy, the insured person receives a certificate of insurance as proof that he or she is insured. Look for these certificates in your spouse's or family member's personal papers, files, and safety deposit box. Nevertheless, even if you can't find any certificates, this doesn't mean your spouse wasn't insured. You should still check with your family member's employer, bank, or such organisation or institution that they belonged to.

Consider the following types of group policies your spouse or family member may have owned.

Employer-Based Group Life Insurance

If your family member was employed at the time of his or

her death, you may be the beneficiary of a life insurance policy issued through his or her employer. Because some employers offer their employees a certain amount of life insurance at no cost, you may not even be aware that your family member was insured by a group policy because he/she did not pay his/her own premiums.

In addition, your family member may have had the option of purchasing additional group life insurance through his/her employer, paying the extra premiums himself/herself. Thus, before assuming that your family member did not have group life insurance, you should check his/her pay slips, and call his/her employer.

Accidental Death Policy

Your relative may have been

offered an accidental death policy through an employer, credit card, or bank. These policies pay benefits if insured individual dies accidentally. This is another type of life insurance you may be unaware that your next of kin had because, occasionally, these policies are offered as part of a loan package, or as a rider to an employer-issued insurance policy. If your family member died accidentally, look for such a policy in his or her files, or contact his or her employer, bank, credit card issuer, or insurance company.

Travel Accident Insurance

If your spouse or family member was killed while travelling in a public transport as a fare-paying passenger, say by air, bus, or train, you may be eligible to receive the proceeds from a travel accident insurance policy he or she may have purchased when buying tickets. In addition, if your family member used a credit card to purchase travel tickets, you may be automatically entitled to a life insurance benefit payable if he or she dies as a result of an accident when using those tickets. Some travel agencies also routinely issue travel accident insurance policies, and employers sometimes pay death benefits to employees who are killed while travelling on company business. Some policies may also include a commuter cover in addition to the basic life cover.

Mortgage Life Insurance

If your family member owned a house, he or she may have

purchased mortgage life insurance or credit life insurance. A mortgage life insurance policy pays off the balance of the policyholder's mortgage upon his or her death. If you're not sure whether your spouse or family member purchased such a policy, check with the bank or mortgage lender or bond holder that financed the house. Sometimes they may have purchased the mortgage life insurance separately from the lender. Such a policy should clear the balance of the loan on the house or property.

Credit life insurance

Banks and finance companies customarily offer credit life insurance when someone takes out a loan. This insurance will pay off the outstanding balance of a loan or account if the insured individual dies. A few extra bucks are added to the monthly loan payments to pay the premiums. Because it is so profitable for the bank or finance company, most institutions sell this type of policy when someone finances a purchase like a car, or signs up for a loan, and they add it to a contract before the individual signs it. Thus, it is likely that you won't find out that your spouse or family member owned such a policy unless you check with credit card companies, banks, or any lenders to whom your family member owed money at the time of his or her death. As long as there was a balance on the loan when they died, don't be quick to settle it using other means, first check whether there was a credit life policy. Even if you may not have the physical documents, the bank should have copies of the contract.

Waiver of Premiums on Death

This is a benefit that is often attached to a non-life or investment policy for a child or a minor. This benefit stipulates that upon death of the payer, the insurance company will carry on as the financier of the premiums until the maturity of the policy. The insurance company will still have to be informed of the death of the payer.

This ensures that minor children don't lose benefits of, for example, education policies that their parents could have taken.

As can be seen, some of the reasons so much money goes unclaimed is precisely because of the above reasons.

If your family member had taken the time to write a last Will and Testament, it is likely that therein would be contained all policies and their numbers, wherever they may have taken them. But if the Will is much older, it does not preclude you from looking in all other places for additional policies that may not have been included in the Will when it was written.

Next, we look at the process of claiming life insurance benefits.

12

The Claiming Process

How do you file a life insurance benefit claim?

Well, as stated before, benefits will not roll out without human intervention. But it is not complicated and you don't necessarily need a lawyer to do this:

The first step is to notify the insurance company that the policyholder has died.
You should contact your insurance agent or the insurance company as soon as possible. You could also call an employer

or bank and ask them to notify the insurance company for you to begin the claims process. Claims from group policies would most likely need to be done via the group administrator, which may be an employer, or a trade union, or any other group.

File a claim form

For death cover and funeral covers, you'll begin the claims process by filling out and signing a number of forms including declaration of identify form, personal medical attendant form, and claimant's declaration form. If you are too distraught to fill out the forms yourself, your insurance agent may fill it out for you, although you'll still have to sign it. If there is another beneficiary named on the policy, that person must also fill out a claim form. To accelerate your claim, follow the insurance company's instructions carefully. Usually documents required include: death certificate, policy document, identity cards of the deceased and those of beneficiaries, and outpatient medical records. Driver's licences would be needed in case of accidental death if the deceased was the driver, as well as post-mortem reports and police reports.

Wait for the company to process the claim. Life insurance claims are usually paid quickly, often within a few days. First, however, the insurance company will ensure that you are the beneficiary of the policy; that the policy is current and in force, and that all conditions of the policy have been met. This is usually a simple matter, and does not delay the claims process. Claims are more often delayed because the insurance company has not received a valid death certificate or all the information requested. As stated above, the insurance company also has a right to challenge or deny a claim if it believes that a policy provision has been violated.

How Should You Receive the Life Insurance Proceeds?

You have a number of options of how you can receive the funds, namely, lump-sum or through a settlement option.

In a lump-sum cash payment
Life insurance proceeds are often paid as lump-sum cash payments. Most people elect this form of payment because it enables them to control how the insurance money is invested or spent.

Through a settlement or instalment option

A settlement or instalment option is a way of paying the proceeds of a life insurance policy other than in a lump-sum cash payment. Many types of settlement options are available, but all are designed to ensure good money management in situations where the beneficiary is unable or unwilling to manage a lump sum of cash. If you receive the proceeds of an insurance policy through a settlement option, the insurance company will keep the policy proceeds, invest them, and pay you interest. Or, you may be allowed to withdraw part of the proceeds or receive periodic payments of both principal and interest.

13

The Life Insurance Professional

It is often said that life insurance is not bought but sold.

That means most people don't wake up one morning and go 'shopping' for insurance. It is often brought to you by a life insurance professional. The fact that not many people go seeking information on life insurance until the agent knocks at the door may explain why so many people know so little about such an important issue. Once you have been alerted about life insurance, for example, after reading this book, you may have a few questions to ask.

Who can sell life insurance? Do I need a Life Insurance professional? Can I do it alone? Is my professional the right person for me? Am I comfortable with him/her?

As you are now aware, life insurance can be a complicated product to purchase. But in this day and age, opportunities abound for do-it-yourself processes through the internet. However, before you go at it alone, you need to consider this:

Why are you buying life insurance? If you're purchasing insurance solely to provide income for your family in the event of your death, you can probably complete this transaction on your own, if you have determined that the rest of your finances are in order. Remember that life insurance is a risk management tool. Unless you know how to carry out your own risk assessment, don't be too quick to think you can do it alone.

Once you have sent in your completed proposal form, the insurance company will tell you what medical tests they need (if any), and you can go to the doctor and have these carried out and submitted to your insurance company, and you will know within a short period of time if your proposal has been accepted.

However, if you are trying to use life insurance for estate planning, business planning, or other complex purposes, you should most probably consult a professional.

If you decide you need professional assistance, you can still do much of the research on your own. The Internet offers a wealth of valuable information. You can learn about different types of life insurance, estimate your life insurance needs using calculators on most companies' websites, and research the financial strength of various insurance companies. All of this can be used as a basis for future discussions with your insurance professional.

Here are some tips to help you in choosing the right professional for this important task:

You may want to interview several insurance agents, but choose only one person to help you. You're better off sticking with just one, rather than having several competing with each other and pressuring you to buy from them.

Licensing: Find out about credentials and experience. If you're going to use a professional, make sure they're qualified to do the job. Licensed professionals subscribe to a code of professional ethics. Many countries have different licensing bodies, and it is important that you check with the relevant authority what the requirements are for a person to be a licensed professional.

There are some international financial service designations such as Certified Financial Planner®(CFP) that may be obvious. There are some localised Professional designations such as Certificate of Proficiency (COP), and Intermediate Certificate in Business Studies (ICBS), and others issued by The Insurance Institute of Southern Africa (ISSA). These qualifications typically mean the person has passed certain licensing exams.

Because insurance is a complicated field, you may want to make sure the person you choose has several years of related experience. (If they are only starting out and you feel comfortable with them, make sure you know their supervisor and that he/she has the necessary qualifications and experience).

A Professional should have knowledge of Personal Finance. The fact that they have passed a regulatory exam and are licensed does not mean that they know the world of personal finance. It is important that they demonstrate knowledge of the field in which they operate. Beyond the products that they sell, they should be able to give you sound advice. They should be able to do important things like risk analysis and needs analysis. Anyone who recommends a product without doing due diligence and finding out your needs and your appetite for risk, may just be a product pusher.

A good professional should be able to explain clear of jargon and complex terminology.

You should never sign an incomplete application form, or let an agent leave to go fill it in in your absence. You are the only one who is responsible for what is on the form, and it is best if it can be in your own hand writing.

Know how your insurance professional is being paid. You don't want someone who is only focused on their commission that they recommend to you only those products that may maximise their profit without due regard for your needs.

There are many different types of fee structures for insurance professionals, including commission only, fee-plus-commission, and fee only. Knowing how your insurance professional is paid will help you evaluate his or her advice and make an unbiased buying decision. Of course, there's nothing wrong with using an insurance professional who earns commissions, but you should know exactly what you're getting for your money.

Find a person you're comfortable working with. You'll be working closely with the person you choose, and disclosing a lot of personal information. Make sure you're dealing with someone you like.

A good professional will also make follow ups from time to time to make sure that your cover is still sufficient as your life changes over time.

Make sure your agent's hours fit your lifestyle. If you typically can't take care of personal business during the week, it will be important to find an insurance professional with evening and weekend hours. Also, find out if other staff members can answer your questions when your agent is unavailable. Know the agency or the brokerage that you are dealing with, and the insurance company that underwrites your policy.

Life insurance is a long-term purchase and it is important to not limit your relationship to the agent that came to you, but to ensure that even if they changed careers and left the industry, you can still get assistance from their company. These are things you need to establish in the beginning of the relationship.

Credit Life Insurance: Good Deal or Rip Off?

What is Credit Life insurance?

When you're borrowing money to buy a house, a car, or a piece of furniture, or applying for a cash loan, it's likely that you'll be asked to purchase credit life insurance. Credit life insurance pays off the balance of your loan should your death or disability precede your loan settlement. But are you getting a good deal?

Banks and financial institutions are virtually the same in any country. When lending money, they want as much security as they can possibly get. The question remains: are you getting a good deal?

"Credit life and disability insurance, also known as "croak and choke," is worthless," States Clark Howard[9] nonchalantly. "It protects the lender if you die or are disabled. It doesn't protect you." He continues. "If you're concerned that your family will lose the house if you die, buy a term life insurance policy that pays your loved ones directly. They can decide how to use the money. Credit life insurance is far more expensive than term life insurance."

That is the view from one side of the coin. The other side will obviously argue that it is better

---

[9] www.clarkhoward.com

for your family to not have to worry about paying for your loans, and not have to lose the goods that you purchased.

Although credit life insurance pays off your loan balance when you die, the first side argues that it's better to purchase term life insurance and cede it to the financial institution, instead of credit life cover. Here's why.

Who Is Protected?

Credit life insurance offers less protection to your loved ones than term insurance

When you purchase credit life insurance, your aim is probably to protect your loved ones. After all, when you die, you'll want them to be able to pay off your debts.

The first problem with credit life cover is that the named beneficiary of your credit life insurance policy is your lender, not your family. When you die, your loved ones don't get the proceeds of your credit life insurance policy - the bank or other lending institution does.

The second problem to consider is the fact that for every loan that you take, you are probably also purchasing a separate credit life insurance whose beneficiary is the provider of that loan. So you could end up with many credit life insurance policies for each one of your loans, thus paying more premiums, without your family being beneficiaries. Your home loan, your car loan, your hire-purchase contract, your cash loan, would all have their own individual credit life policies at various premiums, the sum of which could far exceed a holistic term life insurance policy.

Can I Cede My Term Insurance Policy Instead?

Term insurance policy can be ceded to the lender, and is a much more flexible product since it can be used in a coordinated way to cover all your indebtedness, plus have the balance given to your family or beneficiaries. It better protects your loved ones when you die because your term policy will be used by the financial institution (the cessionary) to clear the debt and pay out the balance of the life cover to the beneficiaries you have named in your policy. Your family can then use that money for whatever they choose.

What else should you know before signing up for credit life insurance?

Here are some other facts about credit life insurance that can help you make an informed decision:

Credit life insurance should be

optional. One fact that your lender may not emphasise is that credit life insurance should be strictly optional - there's no law (in most countries) requiring you to have it.

You should also be able to choose which insurance company you would like to take credit life insurance from. And, you should be able to cancel it at any time if you decide later that you don't want it.

Certain banks and financial institutions have, however, made it policy and a mandatory condition for the granting of a loan or financing. One can understand their need for security especially with unsecured loans. However, the option to cede an existing policy should rather be emphasized rather than taking out a new policy with each loan.

Financial institutions that "tie in" with one underwriter often carry high commissions and are not in the best interest of the consumer. If the lender is "tied in" to one insurance company, it takes away your right to shop for best prices.

Credit life insurance is profitable for lenders. It is so profitable that many banks now have an in-house product that is part of the loan package.

One reason that lenders are anxious to sell credit life insurance is because it's profitable for them to do so. For every policy they sell, they'll receive a commission. In developed countries where clients have an option, banks and other lending institutions often reward their employees for selling credit life insurance and expect them to sell it during loan closing proceedings.

One of the biggest issues to consider is the fact that lenders often add the cost of credit life insurance into your monthly payment amount before closing the loan. If you don't really want it, you could ask them to refigure your loan payment before signing the paperwork. Unfortunately, with some institutions, that will mean no loan! That is how banks flex their financial muscles, ready to knock you out with a rejection, should you not comply.

The financial institution will lend you money you did not require and duly charge you interest on it. This means that if you require a loan for a certain amount, you will be charged a credit life insurance, plus a commission, and in most cases, you may also get charged administration fees. All these are added to the loan amount as debt, and interest is dully charged on the total amount.

They lend you your required amount, plus they lend you the insurance premium, which they duly submit to the insurance company in advance for a year or the term of the loan, and they lend you the commission, which they pocket, and they lend you the administration fee, then charge you interest for the privilege.

If institutions would accept an existing life policy as security, you would not have to pay an additional amount.

This results in the burden of even higher loan repayments and the reduction of the potential loan amount available to borrowers;

Because in most cases credit life insurance is partially treated as group life cover, all borrowers pay the same rate irrespective of their risk profile; and there are inequitable charging structures especially when loans are refinanced.

So, when you sign up for credit life insurance, look for, among others, an institution where proper underwriting procedures are followed so that there is a "balance of risk"; and where there is no compulsory cover, giving you, the borrower a choice to insure and if so, with whom and with what product.

Be sure that your financial institution is not wielding its financial muscles and bullying borrowers into high premium credit life insurance policies because of their unwillingness to assess each borrower's credit risk, and are therefore overcharging everybody for various prevailing conditions such as HIV/AIDS, etc.

There is no argument against having an insurance cover for a liability that may leave your family in financial trouble if you should die before you pay it back. The argument is in the methodology followed to get this cover, and the options available to you to ensure that you get the best premiums for the best cover possible for your individual circumstance.

If you have term life cover with sufficient coverage at reasonable premiums, there is then no need to be paying additional premiums for additional "unnecessary" cover, which will not list your family as beneficiaries.

If, however, you do not have such cover, credit life insurance is a good idea for you, if only you could get best premiums for it.

What If You Repay Your Loan Before Its Term?

Because premiums for credit life are usually paid annually in advance, you should be able to get back the unused premiums for the remainder of the loan term.

Also, be aware that if you are refinancing a loan or consolidating a loan, you are essentially paying off the one loan before its term, albeit with another loan, and are taking a new loan.

Term life insurance premiums, on the contrary are "pay as you go" on a monthly basis.

15

Examples of Ancillary Benefits

Ancillary benefits are those that are dependent, or are attachments to the main policy. It used to be that many of these were not sold as stand-alone policies, but with the changing landscape, many are now stand-alone policies. For example, when you buy a travel ticket, you may also purchase a commuter cover or accidental death cover that would expire at the end of that trip, without having to purchase a full life cover policy.

Let us look at some of those that may largely be ancillary to main life cover, even though under certain circumstances they may stand alone.

ACCIDENTAL DEATH BENEFITS

There are a number of death benefits such as accidental death benefit, commuter cover, or dread disease cover.

As hard as it is to deal with any death, accidental death is more traumatic and very disruptive to life. Children are left as orphans, with relatives who have no means to raise them up.

Death is an enigma; it is never supposed to happen to you, or me but to someone else. Unfortunately, it happens to all.

On our roads there are accidents that take lives and leave others maimed for life.

As far as road deaths are concerned, every road user should take the necessary precautions to preserve life.

Accidental Death Cover

This benefit is payable when the life insured dies as a result of violent, accidental, external and visible means. The benefit amount is usually payable in addition to the basic life cover to which it is attached. In some cases, without any waiting period, there is immediate cover. The terms and conditions may differ from company to company. The benefits could bring much relief when you need it most.

Commuter Cover

As a fare-paying passenger on public transportation, you may not be in control of what is going on, but you should not be helpless. Commuter Cover makes money available for you and your immediate family should death occur on public transport. You can add this cover to your main policy for additional benefits.

Many credit card companies offer this cover automatically when you purchase your tickets with their credit card. Many online travel agents will also offer you a travel insurance not only for your luggage, but for your life as well. While the one purchased for a specific trip would expire at the end of that trip, the one that you add to your insurance policy as an ancillary benefit remains in force as long as you are paying premiums for it.

Your broker will be of assistance to you for more information.

Capital Disability Benefit

Thankfully, not all accidents end in death, but unfortunately, they may leave one disabled for life. This benefit ensures that your quality of life does not deteriorate as a result of disability. The Capital disability benefit will cover you against loss of the ability to perform your own or similar occupation. Like the accidental death cover, it can usually be added to a policy that has a basic life cover, or, in some companies, taken up as a separate insurance cover.

This is usually an age-linked benefit and therefore the premiums increase the older one gets.

Dread Disease Cover

Dread disease insurance also goes by several names such as serious illness or critical illness and covers such issues as cancer, heart attack, stroke, etc. It is important to be clear about what is covered and what is excluded. Sometimes pre-existing conditions may be excluded, or covered at additional premiums. Some conditions may be excluded regardless of whether they're pre-existing or not. If an exclusion(s) is listed, the insurance company will not pay a claim if it can be proven that the illness is as a result of the excluded condition.

Be aware that there may be a requirement for a survival period, which means that the policy will only kick in after a certain number of days after diagnosis, such as 14 days to 28 days.

The policy pays a lump sum which you can use either to supplement your medical aid or spend as you wish.

Bibliography

1. Botha, M, et al, The South African Financial Planning Handbook, LexisNexis, 2016
2. Clason, G.S, *The Richest Man in Babylon,* Signet, 1988
3. https://en.wikipedia.org/wiki/Colin_Bouwer.
4. https://mg.co.za/article/1996-03-08-sabadia-murder-reveals-more-than-just-a-body
5. Letshwene R. N, The Money Field, Moedi, 2015
6. Letshwene R.N, Functional Mastery Over My Finances, Reach Publishers, 2008
7. Letshwene, R. N., Seven Essential Money Skills, Moedi, 2015
8. Masterson, M. Accelerated Program for Six-Figure Copywriting, AWAI, 2001
9. www.7moneyskills.wordpress.com
10. www.clarkhoward.com
11. www.investopedia.com
12. www.miller-miller.com/content/life/life-uw
13. www.moneytips.com/bad-driving-can-affect-your-life-insurance-premiums
14. www.sanlam.co.za
15. www.stamfordadvocate.com/business/moneytips/article/Life-Insurance-Medical-Exams-Going-Away-12123720.php

Other Books by Nelson Letshwene

All these available on www.amazon.com

	***The Money Field*** is like a sports field upon which the game of money is played. In its four quadrants are various players including yourself. Each player's goal is to win. This book gives you the rules, winning strategies and how others play against you. Will you win this game? The money game is life's compulsory game.
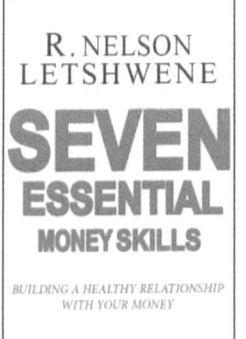	These Money skills are to be installed, activated, and practiced to transform you and your relationship with your money. Learn skills to create multiple streams of income, to save and invest, to protect and build controls, to build long lasting value and to share your bounty with others. Everyone who handles money must have these skills.

This book is a thought stimulator – to get us to think about areas of our financial literacy. You may be good in one but lack in another. Earnings; controls; our psychology of money; debt; savings; investments; assets; etc. Take the journey.

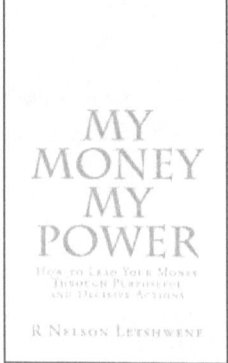

Your money came to you in exchange for your power: be that skill, talent, idea, or sweat. It remains your responsibility to keep that power. It is easy to lose your power to the commercial system and be a slave to lenders and traders. You only retain your power when you turn your money into investments and assets that produce more income. This book is about leading your money through decisive actions to retain your power.

	What is a calling? A Longing; a pining; a wish; a yearning; a hunger; a lust; a craving; an aching, a desire! Life is calling you to live it to the full. The Call will keep ringing until it is answered. Desire is a propensity to grow. Follow the Seven rivers of desire flowing within your being
	The question of what faith is, has kept truth seekers on the path for centuries. Faith is both Art and Science. It is the process of becoming one with your desires and with the creator. Faith is a force in the universe that can make things happen. Purpose if faith with passion. Take this journey now.

THANK YOU

If you enjoyed reading this book, please feel free to leave me a review. Reviews help other readers to know the relevance of the book for them and they help authors like me to improve on our work for the benefit of our readers.

Nelson Letshwene

nelson@moedi.net
@NLetshwene

ABOUT THE AUTHOR

Nelson Letshwene is a speaker and writer with over two decades of experience. He has written and published several books in the field of personal development, motivation and personal finance, as well as in the field of faith and spirituality.

He holds two business degrees and certificates in insurance. He offers courses in personal financial management and continues to be involved in the insurance industry.

He has travelled internationally and continues to hold seminars in the field of personal finance, human development, spirituality, and motivation.

www.nelsonletshwene.com
@NLetshwene

www.ingramcontent.com/pod-product-compliance
Lightning Source LLC
Chambersburg PA
CBHW020425220526
45464CB00002B/565